GROWING
into
GOD

GROWING
into
GOD

EDWINA GATELEY

SHEED & WARD
FRANKLIN, WISCONSIN

As an apostolate of the Priests of the Sacred Heart, a Catholic religious congregation, the mission of Sheed & Ward is to publish books of contemporary impact and enduring merit in Catholic Christian thought and action. The books published, however, reflect the opinions of their authors and are not meant to represent the official position of the Priests of the Sacred Heart.

A SHEED & WARD BOOK
ROWMAN & LITTLEFIELD PUBLISHERS, INC.
Published in the United States of America
by Rowman & Littlefield Publishers, Inc.
A wholly owned subsidiary of The Rowman & Littlefield Publishing Group, Inc.
4501 Forbes Boulevard, Suite 200, Lanham, Maryland 20706
www.rowmanlittlefield.com

PO Box 317
Oxford
OX2 9RU, UK

British Library Cataloguing in Publication Information Available
Library of Congress Cataloging-in-Publication Data

Gateley, Edwina.
    Growing into God / Edwina Gateley.
      p. cm.
    ISBN 1-58051-080-9 (alk. paper)
    1. Christian poetry, American.
    PS3557 .A859 G7 2000
    813'.54—dc21   00-033884
Printed in the United States of America

♾ The paper used in this publication meets the minimum requirements of American National Standard for Information Sciences—Permanence of Paper for Printed Library Materials, ANSI/NISO Z39.48-1992.

To Jean Lavin, OSB,
and all who participate in
Stillpoint Retreats.
May you never cease
to grow into God.

CONTENTS

Introduction *xi*

I CONCEPTION

Awakening *3*
Deeps *4*
Untitled *5*
Edge *6*
Intrusion *7*
Control *8*
God Light *9*
Silence *10*
Harmony *11*
Dryness *12*
Waiting *13*

II GESTATION

Cycles *17*
Faith *18*
Train *19*
Loss *21*
Fall *23*
Prayer *24*
Desert *25*
Expectant *26*

III Birthing

Water *31*
Woven *32*
Earth Child *33*
Son *34*
Mama *35*
Little Things *36*
Listen *37*
Wisdom *38*
Diminishment *39*
Wish *40*
Presence *41*
Pursuit *42*

IV Dying

Nothing *45*
Vision *46*
Night *47*
Stirrings *48*
Sitting *49*
Betrayal *50*
Dam *51*
Mission *52*
Cave *54*
Dying *55*
The Guide *56*
Spaces *57*
Farewell *58*
Journey *60*

V HOME

Home *65*
Reflection *66*
Reunion *67*
Incarnation *68*
Deeply Grateful *69*
Ground *70*
Full Circle *71*
We Are *75*

Introduction

A s a child I discovered God. Or, more realistically, I stumbled upon the God who first invited me to play. In my younger years, my relationship with the Divine was gloriously intimate, playful, and very, very special. Our deep friendship was, like many childhood friendships, filled with whispers, secrets, and adventures. God was my first, best playmate.

But as time passed, my friendship with God gradually took on a different form through the mediation of teachers and clergy. Insistent teachings about God, who was Father and Judge in heaven and who had created me to get to know him, love him, and serve him, gradually took hold in my formative religious understanding. Sin, guilt, failure, and suffering all began to take on a major role in my changing awareness of God.

Like a parent-child relationship, my journey with God was full of ups and downs, a roller coaster,

touching heights of love and joy, and depths of despair and anger; rarely was the ongoing battle to
love and be loved simply static. Never was it bor-
ing. But it was always and most definitely about the
"Other"; it was always focused on a very definite
being outside of myself. As such, I could choose to
direct my passions or problems or concerns at my
God-figure. I could *talk to* this God; *negotiate with*
this God; even *gaze at* symbols of this God in holy
places. Such a God was not all that difficult to deal
with—given that I could choose to speak, look at,
or call upon him according to my particular needs
and fancy at any given time. I also could also choose
simply to ignore this distant being at whim.

My problem with God began when, quite unbidden, this very same God *shifted position*! It all
began as I spent more and more time in silent prayer,
reflected more deeply on my life experiences, and
began to read more of the writings of the mystics. A
seed of discomfiting doubt was sown in my very guts:
if what I was reading of the mystics was right (and
deep down I suspected it was), then God was im-
possibly, frighteningly close! Such a growing
awareness brought back memories of my childhood
relationship with God—intimate and playful—but
long since, along with my toys, consigned to his-
tory. It felt as if God were sneaking back into my
life as in my childhood—secretly—with whispers,
secrets, and surprises. No longer at some comfort-
able, distant place that allowed for negotiation,
debate, and withdrawal if so required, God, it

appeared, had actually taken up abode in my territory, in my very being.

Meister Eckart's audacious declaration, "God is at home, it is we who have gone out for a walk," haunted me. Not only did it haunt me but, in my deepening moments of silence, I began to sense an inner stirring that dared validate such a sentiment. It was all very distressing. If God, indeed, was *that* close, if God, indeed, was *at home within me*, then my whole system of divine communication—a lifetime of well learned prayers, rituals, and entreaties, all addressed to an External Deity—would no longer fit. A whole system of communication was losing ground—much more scary and discomfiting than the transition from letter writing to e-mail.

I was devastated. Who had I been talking "to" and "at" all these years? Had it all been wasted and irrelevant? I felt betrayed by my own dedication. God (outside) had been my life's guide to whom I had given my all—a relationship based on certainty. Now that certainty was being questioned as God's place in the universe (my universe) was beginning to shift.

Much of the poetry and writing in this book reflects that shifting and the real struggle to remain faithful in the face of radical changes to beliefs I had harbored my entire life.

Betrayal, insecurity, and loss are all part of the deepening process of faith by which we come, ultimately, to whisper our assent to the amazing reality of God—in us. Our "yes" is an acknowledgment and acceptance of the miraculous call to each one of us to grow into God. It is a moment of conversion—a terrifying fall into the God in us—when at last, after centuries of separation and distance from the Holy, we dare to believe in the incarnation of God in our very selves. Such humbling, joyful, and liberating awareness is not for the spiritually fearful. Rather, it is for those who believe in the words of Jesus: "Those who love me will keep my word; and [God] will love them, and we shall come to them and make our home with them" (John: 14:23).

Like the cocoon that houses the beauty of a butterfly, we will struggle in darkness and with doubts. Ultimately, however, if we truly believe in our call to wholeness, we will emerge through our spiritual journey brilliant and shining as a new creation.

From the withered tree, a flower blooms.

—*Shoyo Roku*

I

Conception

Awakening

Awakening,
I thank you, God,
for the blessing of this day,
for pushing life
that stirs beneath my feet,
for the birds
that swoop in joy
at the breaking of the earth
and the giddy dancing
of new leaves.

Awakening,
I stand, awed,
at the echoing
of your word—
tumbling down
the gold-red mountain,
roaring in the rising waters—
waiting to be heard.

Awakening,
I bless you, God,
for abundant life
poured out extravagant,
in riotous splendor
before our shuttered eyes,
and for the leaping creation
around our still deep slumbering.

Deeps

The water is deep in places
and very very still,
though little streams
constantly splash
along its edges
and dozens
of tiny water creatures
skim and slide
at play
upon the surface.
But I can see
into the deep
where all lies silent
and untouched.
And I can see,
reflected there,
beneath the giddy surface,
golden stones
lit by the sun,
shimmering
and, oh, so clear,
proclaiming God's wisdom,
transparent and eternal,
shining beneath our feet.

Untitled

God is lonely
for our longing.

Edge

It is safe by the edge
where the curling foam
falls into tiny bubbles.
Here I can walk
undisturbed by the depths,
unafraid of sinking
and dark silences.
Here, by the edge,
I can dance and sport,
leaving in the salt sand
only slight indents
where my feet barely touched.
Here, by the edge,
I can quietly watch,
musing only
on how it must be
to be seized and swept
by the deep embrace—
ever calling my name.

Intrusion

Living God,
Passionate One,
don't seize me
in the night,
nor clasp me
in your great embrace
whilst sleep
still holds me tight.

Living God,
Passionate One,
wait till
the silvery dawn
dispels the deep
in which I sleep
that I might flee
alone.

Control

Perhaps, if I tread quietly,
the shadows will not see me,
and I shall creep around them—
soul screaming for the light.

If open wide I keep my eyes,
the night will not absorb me,
and I shall lock the sun
in my unblinking gaze.

If I chant out loud my litanies,
the silence will not seize me,
and I will hear the comfort
of my own proud song.

If I grasp my treasures tightly—
filling every little space—
there'll be no room for me to make
an empty place for God.

God Light

The sky is washed
in transparent gold,
holding aloft
the setting sun.
All is bathed in light.
Even dark corners
are set ablaze,
naked and surprised,
in sudden moments
of glory.

So too,
does God's light
play over us
in unceasing flow,
its brilliance reducing
our deepest darkness
into a passing shadow,
scuttling away
before God's awesome grace.

Silence

I feel the silence hears me,
waits for me,
and I am conscious
of intrusion.
Will she receive me,
swallow me,
absorb me,
so that I too,
become silence?
Or will I dally
with her,
maintaining separateness,
refusing
to become lost
in her great
and gaping spaces?
Will I flee her emptiness
and stumble,
relieved,
into my waiting car
and the secure comfort
of roaring engine?
I flee.

Harmony

Thank you, God,
for quiet time
beside the water,
listening to the murmur
of ever flowing
ebb and tide,
the leaping forward,
the pulling back,
eternally harmonious.

I, too,
must learn to flow,
allow myself to fall
and be immersed
in deep waters,
that I may know
the joy of rising up
and being thrust,
trusting,
to new and distant edges.

Dryness

Like a sponge,
dried up and brittle,
I wait,
longing to be soaked,
softened, and
made heavy
by God—
Eternal reservoir.

I wait
ever vigilant
to the first stirrings
of new consciousness,
ever longing
to be filled and swelled
by God in me,
utterly conscious,
in my emptiness,
of my destiny.

Waiting

I need simply and only
to wait upon God
without expectation,
and God,
all longing,
resting in me,
will breathe
in me
the music
of my soul.

II

Gestation

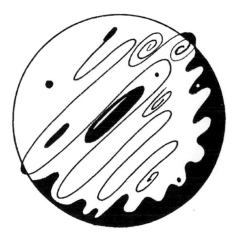

Cycles

It is spring.
The earth beneath my feet
is moist and heavy
with dampness,
pulsing to break into life.
But in me
there is a winter,
bleached and barren.
It was not always so.
And as I sit,
benumbed
in winter's spaces,
observer of life's cycles,
I must remember
that there was once in me,
a spring,
and it must come again.

Faith

When all around is deadened gray,
help me, God,
keep on believing.
When dulled my soul,
though the song birds sing,
help me, God,
keep on believing.
When even I
dare doubt your grace,
help me, God,
keep on believing.
When dreams collapse
and bright hopes die,
help me, God,
keep on believing.

Train

Sitting on the subway train
shuddering its way
through the city of Chicago,
I saw the gang graffiti,
defiant and bold,
painted on the warehouse walls—
words of anger and violence—
screaming at the blank eyes
of innocent passengers
mindlessly staring out
through grubby windows.
And there,
in bright red,
surrounded by gang symbols,
four words stood large and bold:
"I LOVE YOU, MAMA."
My heart grieved
for unspoken story,
for the angry son who,
in the midst
of an act of rage,
remembered he loved his mama
and needed to tell
the world.
I hurt for his mama
the other woman,
who wept and prayed

that her son, so well beloved,
would be safe,
that her God,
ridiculously,
miraculously,
would raise him up
whole and healed.
And in the train, rocking,
I dreamed with her,
that God slipped through
graffitied walls and,
hot with a mother's love,
plucked up
and raised so high,
so gloriously,
the son
she loved so well.

Loss

I do not know you, God.
I thought I did—
your attributes were listed long
in my divine inventory.
At school I learned
of where you lived
and what you did
and why you made us
in the first place.
We got graded
for reciting your commands—
(writ in stone they said—
in ancient times).
You were comforting then, God,
like a big parent
watching out for me,
whom I longed to please
and feared to betray.
Until one day,
a grayness fell upon my world,
like a shroud,
choking my hymns and prayers.
Though I called on you,
there was no answer,
no cloud by day nor fire by night,
only a terrible silence
screaming your absence—

leaving me,
not knowing,
my deep, deep faith
disintegrating
floating away like ashes
on a night breeze,
dissipating in the darkness,
leaving me all hollowed out.

Fall

I was a kite.
I flew high and free,
dallying in the tallest tree.

Now I am grounded,
sorely torn,
fallen back where I was born.

Brought steep down
from my giddy flight
to tremble in my ground's dark night.

Prayer

The wind shrieks—
mocking the silence in my heart,
and everything that moves around me
beckons me to rise and play.
"There is nothing here!"
murmur insistent voices.
You are forgotten—
left behind
from humanity's swelling dance.
Alone you sit—
postured all correct,
awaiting the divine encounter
and meeting only
your empty self
staring back
in mild amusement
at your longing.

Desert

Ah, what is it
that impels me flee the sun
and the whirlings of the day
to fall upon myself
in solitude?
Then, so accustomed to rising,
my soul—newly timid—
hovers on the edge of fall,
bewildered by the shadows
and beset with a thousand voices
calling me back
from the brutal journey
to return to the giddy dance
of bright consciousness,
bidding me leave
this dry volcanic desert
full of pitfalls and sharp rocks
that wound my tender spirit.
The voices, the memories,
and many fleeting thoughts
depend for their survival
on my return from deep ground
and vast emptiness,
for there, in that space,
there is no dance
nor whirling days awash in sun,
nothing lives,
but emptiness.

Expectant

Sitting, stilled,
awaiting
the breath of God
to course through me—
quickening my expectant soul
with new fresh grace—
ah, so longed for!
Sitting breathing gently,
steadily, correctly—
a fitting welcome
for divinity.
But, ah,
where are you, God?
Where the spinning rush
of joy
settling in the pit of my being—
sure sign
of favored presence?
Where the deep pulsating peace,
(born only of the Other)
that gentles my very essence?
Yet still I sit
like an empty shell
demanding fullness,
longing for completion.
Ah, God,
will you burst within me,
unexpected,

and dizzy me with your presence?
Or must I sit,
quietly broken
forever longing—forever open,
like a mother
awaiting her term?

III

Birthing

Water

I listen to the water
washing oh so softly
upon the rocks and stones
strewn upon the beach.
And, as I listen
to the constant rhythm,
I know that God,
in unending desire,
so washes over us,
desirous to soak and moisten
dry spaces and hard edges,
never ceasing, never pausing,
only changing rhythm,
in the constant pursuit
of gathering us in
the great embrace.

Woven

There is a divinity
spilt over the earth
that flows where
we don't see
and clothes
all dead and living things
in mantles of eternity.
Though in our gray
and stressed out world
we miss the holy thing,
still it shines,
wove fast and deep
in our dark humanity.

And if one day
we'd dare to glance
into a child's wide wondrous eyes,
we'd see reflected,
shining there,
God's bright inviting dance.

Earth Child

The earth is yours, young son.
Its great round beauty circles you,
awaiting your first touch.

The earth beckons you, little one,
into the caverns of its towering cities
and down the labyrinths of its myriad ways
lit by orange light.

The earth awaits you, little one,
to fall, all zealous, into its heart,
catch you up in its pounding beat
and absorb the sun in your eyes.

The earth cries for you, little son,
dreaming that your fresh glad spirit
will heal its gaping wounds
and renew its running waters with your tears.

The earth is yours, little one,
to halt the raping of its woods,
cleanse the skies of foul winds,
and turn its dust to rich black soil.

The earth needs you, little son,
like a weary mother, long languishing,
waiting the arms of her child
to wreath her round with bright new dreams.

Son

"Mama," my child breathed,
all expectant and wide eyed.
"If you were a mama whale
and I was a baby whale
and a whole bunch of fierce sharks
came to attack me,
what would you do?"
"Son," I answered fiercely,
"I would thrash my tail
and charge at those sharks
so fast and furiously
they would swim away in terror!"
"Mama," my son continued, eyes shining,
"Would you hide me
under your fin?"
"Son," I replied,
"I would keep you tight close
to my tummy,
nothing would dare touch you."
"Mama," my son insisted,
"What if one of those sharks
circled and attacked me from underneath?"
"Son" I answered,
"I would do a huge underwater somersault
and whack him on the nose with my tail."
"Mama," my son whispered, breathless,
"Mama—I love you."

Mama

I did not know
how fiercely
a child could squeeze and loose
my heart.
I did not know
how deeply
his sudden, momentary absence
could chill my guts.
And I did not truly know
the passion
of God's love
for me
until a child slipped
into my life
and called me "mama."

Little Things

I watch the waves
surge and suck
in wild motion.
I hear the great rising up,
the tumbling forward,
and the thud of watery force
upon the rocks.
But if I stand
against the wind
and listen deeply
to the ebb,
my soul catches
the whispered hush
of breaking bubbles
beneath the mighty crashing,
and I become aware
of little things
that hide and play
in joy
beneath the roaring
of the great.

Listen

It is not my business
to seek enlightenment
or holiness;
mine only
to listen to the wind
caressing all creation,
to be awed
at the tumbling of the waters
soaking all dried things;
mine only
to delight
in the song of the bird
and be attentive
to the rhythmic beating
of the earth
beneath my feet;
mine only
to receive with love
all that rises to meet me
at the dawn
of each new day.

Wisdom

They stretched beyond my sight—
millions of tiny pebbles,
broken stones, and smooth rocks
thrown together,
heaped, it seemed,
in careless huddles,
then washed apart
and rushed to new places
to nudge against
other, different shapes,
falling together
in patterns ever changing.
But over all,
in never-ceasing constancy,
flowed the great water,
drenching and shifting
great and small,
stretching out
in wondrous unfolding
of Wisdom's great design.

Diminishment

To the degree that we
are broken and wounded—
so is God.
As the earth sickens and shrivels
through neglect and greed—
so does God.
As the little ones hunger
and are trampled upon—
so is God.
As more are imprisoned
and starved of light—
so is God.
So will God
be diminished
and hidden from us,
until—
deeply wounded—
we dare rise
from our dying
and, groaning mightily,
break open
our dark and tiny hearts
in the Spirit's new birthing.

Wish

Sometimes I wish
that God had made
my heart of steel,
so that pain would not
slip through
and grip me
so unkindly.
Sometimes I wish
that God, like a magician,
would sweep upon us
and banish all our darkness.
Sometimes I wish
that God had simply
made us angels
and left us
to play harps
and fly around,
cocooned in cotton ball clouds.
Sometimes I wish
that God would hurt, too,
or long to run away
or have misgivings . . .

Then I am overwhelmed
for I know,
that in my heart
not made of steel,
God is also me.

Presence

See there,
amidst the strewn garbage,
a tiny perfect shell,
so intricately formed,
so delicate in shape,
lodged within
our washed up debris,
whispering loveliness
right in the garbage,
its very being
urging wisdom
by its lone persistent presence
within the broken.

Pursuit

I do not pursue God—
God pursues me,
hungering in my deeps
for my momentary glance
inadvertently cast
when I'm caught and held—
ah, so briefly—
by divine aching
in my guts.
I do not know
when God will seize me so
in unexpected pause,
only that it will pass
like a lover's touch
brushing against my flight
at dusk,
leaving me
unfilled,
unknown,
and unsurrendered.

IV

Dying

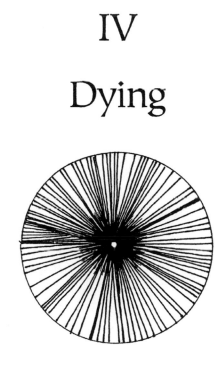

Nothing

I must come to understand
what it means
to hold on to nothing—
it is the ultimate
experience of faith.
There is nothing left,
only God,
only God
and me—
my little self
in God.

Vision

Like a white moon
hung in a blackened sky
my vision shone—
clear and splendid.
Ah, how I loved it,
romanced and treasured it.
How I traced it lovingly,
caressed it and proclaimed it.
And all beheld
my vision clear
like a white moon
against night suspended.
But slowly
and so stealthily,
shadows slid across
my well-loved vision
until it was no more
like a white moon
brightening
all it shone upon,
but only a night—
cold and comfortless.
How I grieve!
Oh! How I grieve
my vision
shadowed over.

Night

The dark night of the soul
is not a desperate falling
into a state
of darkness and despair.
It is, rather,
a monotonous plodding
along an even, unremarked path,
devoid of startling falls
and sharp edges
or anything that might arouse
a spirited response.
The dark night of the soul
is a gray pedestrian place which,
in its very bleakness,
slowly eats at passion
and vitality,
leaving one aware only
of insignificance.

Stirrings

I tremble
before your longing,
echoing in the cosmos,
lonely God;
and I am disturbed
by your gentle expectancy
that I might glance your way.
I resist
your restless stirring
lodged deep and unbidden
in my soul;
yet I ache
in the still, dark hours
to fall, surrendered,
into your patient waiting.

Sitting

Just in the act
of sitting
receptive and still—
just in the desiring
to pray—
is the moment
of grace.
Just in the small attention
given to letting go
is the dying itself.
For God delights
in my desiring
and is content
with my restlessness.
God sits
with my nothing,
gently loving me
in it all.

Betrayal

Where are you, God?
I scratch around for you
in dried-up ground,
like a hen
seeking grain.
Clouds of dust rise up
before me
and shadow
the hunger in my eyes.
And I am left
bereft
in this gray place,
bewildered
at the betrayal
of your absence.

Dam

God's grace
is like a great dam
held back
within us,
and God,
a longing mother,
waiting to break open
and immerse us
in her waters.

Mission

Sometimes I remember,
in a hushed moment,
the daring of my youth,
all I claimed
and gathered in,
built up
and spread out—
casting the word of God
all over the world
in a great young surge
of mission zeal.

Sometimes I remember,
in a hushed moment,
the thousands of miles
I traveled,
crossing mountains,
desert and bushland
to far distant peoples,
inspiringly different
and gloriously colorful.

Sometimes I remember,
in a hushed moment,
how they molded me,
giving me new voice
and a deeper vision,

leaving me lonely
amongst my own.

Sometimes I remember,
in a hushed and sacred moment,
how my small familiar God
slipped from my hold
like a doll,
as I stumbled,
gasping,
into the divine expanse.

Cave

There is a cave in me
resting in ancient shadows
deeper than movement,
undisturbed by light and sound.

There is a cave in me
tucked into dark silence,
eternally beckoning
and waiting to be known.

There is a cave in me
cast before time began,
filled with divine store
ever deepening in sweetness.

There is a cave in me
and daunting is its path,
tenderly and insistently
whispering for my dying.

Dying

There is nothing dramatic
in the death of God.
Just a slow, inexorable
shifting of ground
beneath my solid stand.
Just a growing gut awareness
that it is all going—
icons, books, bells, and creeds—
the comforting images
that once were the pattern
and substance of my life,
(forever mine, it seemed)
now dissolve
in a mist of memories
falling, irretrievable,
behind me,
like toys well loved
but abandoned,
to dissolve in passing shadows.
Will I die, too,
along with my trinkets of the divine?
Will I dissolve also,
into the sands
that shift beneath me?

Or will the earth
gather me and hold me—
nursing new and sturdier seeds.

The Guide

And why
did you snatch from me
my land and home,
creeping upon me so subtly,
and I entranced
by the light in your eyes?
And why did I,
submissive and screaming,
let go my grasp
of my own mansions
and fireside hearth?
And why,
like Kali—
ancient goddess of the dying—
did you peel back
the turf of the underworld,
beckoning me
into the dark, moist earth,
alone?

Spaces

My God died
and left me rootless,
floating like a shadow
without a home—
no place to snuggle down
safe and warm
like a nesting bird.
In a moment,
it seemed,
all my gathered
little twigs
and well-placed branches
fell apart,
leaving spaces
I had never known
and a great hollowness
in my belly.
My God died,
leaving me
orphaned.

Farewell

And if I whisper "Farewell"
to you, my God,
who will take your place?
Who will fill
the great cathedral
where I found
and cherished you
with such delight?
And who
will feed me, God,
when you are gone?
Who will give me
sacred mysteries
shrouded in awe?
Who will sing
those hymns
that carried my soul
into a place of sweetness?
And who,
oh who, my God,
will hold my hand
as I turn from this,
my family,
to take an untrod path?
If I whisper "Farewell,"
will the great marble pillars
and frescoed walls

crumble and fall upon me?
Will they crush,
in outrage,
my brave, bewildered spirit?
What if softly,
stealthily, and oh,
yes—so softly—
I bid my last farewell
unnoticed
and slip
into the night?

Journey

Ah, here it is,
in this small, secret place—
all that I now have
hidden in a handful
of poems and memoirs—
my life fitting nicely
in my desk drawer.
You did so much,
the shadows say,
built little kingdoms,
loved the poor,
and was applauded
by the rich.

They kept on growing—
my little kingdoms—
in ways beyond my arts.
And so I left them,
weeping as a mother
leaving her children—
deep adored, but grown.

Now I have my papers
and my memories,
and I may claim my pride
in what was done
and left behind.

But I must no longer
watch the blank horizon,
dreaming for sight or sound
of child come home.
I must now
to my own return,
and where she is,
there must make my home.

V

Home

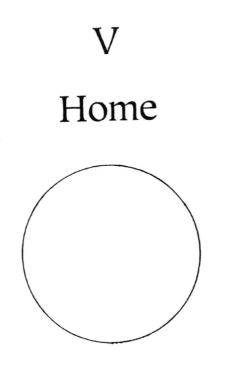

Home

Home
is where I no longer
need seek,
I am simply there,
come to rest
after frenzied journeyings
and circlings,
passionate pursuits,
rising and falling.
One day,
bleak wind
battering at my door,
I gently close it,
knowing I must,
and watch the wild cacophony
I have loved
fall away
behind me
into the graying horizon,
sweeping my tears
into the waters
and singing my songs
to the universe,
now forever changed
by my passage—
not glancing back—
having brought me
safely home.

Reflection

There is buried within us
a beauty hidden so deep
that we would think
it would forever sleep.
But there are those,
whose eyes so luminous shine,
they reflect upon our universe
the light of the Divine.

Reunion

Wake, small soul,
and dare believe
that God,
like a willing prisoner—
harboring secret sweetness—
sits rooted
in my being,
waiting for
the ridiculous in faith
to fall into
the inner chasm,
(milky with God
and flowing with honey),
there to find,
small soul,
that I am lost
when God,
Eternal Seeker,
is found
and leaps from within me
to run free
and passionately,
scattering joy
and juiciness
on all the dried-up earth.

Incarnation

Breathing slowly,
constant, calming rhythm
halting aimless thought,
inviting life's gentle grace
to flow,
I am,
but for a second,
held and entranced
by a consciousness,
incisive and certain,
of God
nesting in my deeps,
and I—
forever mother.

Deeply Grateful

When I stopped waiting
and only sat,
breathing gently, steadily,
lost simply
in the flow of air . . .
Ah, then,
you tumbled, God,
like an avalanche
fast falling
within me,
gathering self-energized force,
unexpected, unrequested,
but suffusing and possessing all—
leaving me
stunned,
stilled,
and deeply grateful.

Ground

I must creep very quietly
in this space
for it is unfamiliar
and leaves me feeling
like an intruder
on Another's Ground.
But this is not so—
no intruder am I.
My deepest self knows,
in soundless awe,
that this
is my ground,
and that this,
my ground,
is God.

But hush, quiet now,
lest I flee
in disbelief,
for I am not yet home
in God.
Hush, quiet now, until
in the lengthening
hours of night,
I make my home
here
in this sacred place.

Full Circle

I knew you, God,
when I was but a child—
a little thing,
carried aloft, it seemed,
by clouds of ecstasy;
borne along each day
by the thundering
of your feet
circling me,
teaching me
steps and dances magical.
Ah, I loved to creep,
breathless and adoring,
into the dark and musty church
where all my childhood secrets
spilt upon your breast
as I vowed to you
my life—
and death.

Ah, God,
I was but a child
when I discovered you
and knew,
with a child's
passionate, loyal conviction,
that you were real.
You were my playmate—

sporting round the marble pillars,
my champion
ever standing by my side.
My Mother—
circling me in deep compassion.
You were my Father—
strong, protective.
And my Beloved—
in whom I was wove.

I was but a child,
but I found you, God.
I crept upon you
with giggles and delight,
awestruck
by your presence
and by your mystery.
Fiercely, I bound myself
to you—
so long ago,
dressed in school uniform.
No fire burned
so deep and hot
as my young love for you.
Never, I swore,
would I betray this passion.
It was not betrayal,
nor new fire or passion,

that muted your bright light—
it was me,
leaving behind my child
and all her awe and mystery
for reason, logic, and debate,
loosening the fixed and awestruck gaze
to ponder, instead,
the intricacies of your ways.
The whispers of my girlhood
turned into chants and litanies;
the giggles and delight—
left in disgrace
on the great stone steps
of your dwelling place.

My dance was lost
to pilgrimage.

But your dance
never ceased, God.
Still you circled waiting—
to play and whisper
once again.
Enchant me
with your deep sweet silence
and take up our dance
once stilled.

And as my life full circled sweeps,
again I see the magic spaces;
and in my deep imagining,
I hear your whispered breathing—
urging delight and play.
And the spilling of your secrets—
extravagant—
upon my breast.
Gathering now your treasures,
hidden so deep and long
within myself—
I know you, God,
and I am but a child—
come Home.

We Are

Do not wait for me
nor expect me.
Do not seek me
nor hope for me.
All is ready.
All is complete.
All is here.
All is now.
We are.